C000070315

WHISKY

The Connoisseur's
Companion

WHISKY

The Connoisseur's
Companion

Cover: Distilling apparatus,
from a 16th-century print.

First published in Great Britain in 1999 by
PAVILION BOOKS LIMITED
London House, Great Eastern Wharf
Parkgate Road, London SW11 4NQ

Copyright © 1995 Nardini Editore, Fiesole (FI), Italy
Text by Patrizia Cantini
English translation © Pavilion Books Limited 1999

A CIP catalogue record for this book is available
from the British Library.

ISBN 1 86205 324 3

Set in Times New Roman
Printed in Italy

2 4 6 8 10 9 7 5 3 1

This book can be ordered direct from the publisher.
Please contact the Marketing Department.
But try your bookshop first.

THE STORY
OF WHISKY

Let other poets raise a fracas
"Bout vines, an' wines, an' drucken Bacchus,
An' crabbit names an' stories wrack us,
An grate our lug:
I sing the juice Scotch bear can mak us,
In glass or jug.

Scotch Drink, 1785
Robert Burns

Origins

Distillation is an ancient skill whose origins to a great extent remain to be discovered and deciphered. But *most* experts seem to agree that it originated in the Far East in about the 9th century BC. At the start, distillation was a science practised exclusively by Arab chemists who used it to make perfumes and medicinal drugs. The words "alcohol" and "alembic" (the ancient word for a still) are derived respectively from the Arabic *al-kuhl*, which means "very fine powder to colour the eyebrows black", and *al-anbiq*, which means "vessel". But it was not until the process of distillation was introduced into Europe that the first drinkable spirits were developed.

But other mysteries shrouded the initial development of distillation. While it may be accepted that distillation reached Europe by way of Egypt, it is more difficult to establish with certainty the date when this happened. Nevertheless, it would not be far from the truth to say that distillation of strong liquor from wine or cereals was already widespread in Europe during the early Middle Ages; indeed it had already been mentioned in the 6th century by the Welsh poet Taliesin in the *Mead Song*.

However, one must wait a little longer before one can talk of whisky itself. This is in spite of the fact that according to Irish legend it was St Patrick, the Roman-British missionary who brought Christianity to Ireland in the 5th century, who imported the art of distillation from the Mediterranean region to the Celtic island. But in response to this legend the Scots maintain that St Patrick was born in the town of Dumbarton in Scotland, and that it is therefore they who could lay claim to the invention of the miraculous drink. So for centuries the Irish and the Scots have competed for this title, the former claiming that whisky was invented in Ireland and travelled from there to Scotland, while the latter claim exactly the opposite.

It is now generally accepted that whisky was first developed in Ireland – although when speaking of Irish "whisky" it is more correct to use the spelling "whiskey". The name now used all over the world to describe

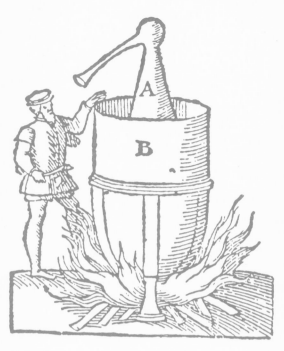

this liquor comes from Gaelic, the word "whisky" being derived from the Gaelic *uisge* (or *uisce*) *beatha*, meaning "water of life". There are at least two other different spellings of the same expression, which probably indicate an early stage in the term's evolution: *usquebaugh* and *uisgebaugh*. It is from the first part of this word (pronounced *ui-sca-ba*) that the modern word "whisky" is derived, and as already mentioned it is spelt "whiskey" by the Irish.

But it was not actually the Irish who were responsible for the corruption of the Gaelic word. The word "whiskey" first came to be used by the British soldiers who invaded

Ireland in the course of the 12th and 13th centuries to conquer the island. According to the Irish historian Malachy Magee, Henry II's soldiers discovered the delights of the local spirit, and they called it "whiskey" because they found it hard to pronounce the Gaelic word. Henry II's army invaded Ireland in 1172, by which time the first distilleries had been set up and whiskey was already widely known and appreciated all over that country. Originally restricted

to monasteries, the distillation of drinkable alcohol from cereals had become a nationwide activity. It was speedily exported all over England as a result of its great popularity with the soldiers of the Crown.

But whiskey was not officially introduced to the English court until the 16th century, when the Earl of Cork, an Irish nobleman, presented no less than thirty-two gallons (over 140 litres) of the precious spirit to Queen Elizabeth I and Sir Walter Raleigh; as a result the earl was branded a traitor by many in his country. Traitor or not, the Earl of Cork's gift led to a great increase in the import of whiskey into

England and it marked the beginning of its success throughout Europe and the world.

Whiskey and whisky

Before Elizabeth I had tasted Irish whiskey, the Scots were already distilling whisky from malted barley. The first written reference to this practice can be found in a Scottish Exchequer register of 1494: "Eight *bolls* of malt for brother John Corr to make aqua vitae" (a boll was an ancient cereal measure). Whiskey had remained an exclusively Irish product at least until the end of the 12th century, but it was then introduced into Scotland where the local population learned to produce it, and they gradually made changes to the original recipe. The Scots introduced a new element into the manufacture of their whisky: peat. A combustible fossil derived from partially decomposed vegetable matter saturated with water, peat is abundant in both Ireland and Scotland. The Irish preferred coal to fire the kilns in which the malted barley was dried, while the Scots always favoured peat as a fuel,

the result being to give the distillate its unmistakable aroma of smokiness which is still such a dominant characteristic of Scotch whisky today.

Apart from this, the method used to produce Scotch whisky was at first much the same as that used for Irish whiskey, and at least until the middle of the 19th century only malted barley was used in both Ireland and Scotland. However, the introduction of a heavy new tax on malt forced Irish distillers to add a certain amount of "raw" barley to the barley malt. The result of this blend was so popular that even when the British government abolished the tax on malt, the Irish continued to make their whiskey using a proportion of unmalted barley.

Whisky's initial development in Scotland was connected with its medicinal properties, to such an extent that in 1505 the Guild of Surgeon Barbers in Edinburgh acquired the monopoly for its distillation. But from the mid-16th century onward, lawsuits arising from the many violations of this privilege became increasingly frequent, because whisky was becoming established as a drink in itself, rather than just as a medicine. In 1579 the Scottish Parliament was obliged to restrict the privilege of distillation to the aristocracy because all over the country there was no longer enough barley to feed the people. Distillation was already widespread, often being a family business.

Even so, throughout the 16th century and for a long time after, the word "whiskey" remained synonymous with Ireland, as is shown in the following lines from *The Malcontent*, a tragi-comedy written by John Marston in 1604:

The Dutch are drunkards,
The Danes have blond hair,

*The Irish have usquebaugh
And the French have syphilis.*

The whiskey imported by the English was Irish, while the whisky made in Scotland was drunk exclusively in Scotland. This was partly because of the strong peaty aroma of Scotch whisky, and it was only in the 18th century that it began to be imported by England. By then whisky had been the national drink of the Scottish subjects of the Stuart rulers for many years. This is clear from the *Bannatyne Manuscript*, an anthology of ancient Scottish poetry produced in 1568: it contains a poem entitled *Why sowld not Allane honorit be* ("Why should Allan not be honoured"), which sings the praises of Allane o'Maut, or Allan the Malt, a popular personification of the cereal used to make whisky.

In the 18th century the celebrated Scottish poet Robert Burns wrote *The Ballad of John Barleycorn*, based on an ancient Scottish song, which shows how deeply whisky is rooted in Scottish tradition. Throughout the 17th century, Irish whiskey and Scottish whisky continued to develop independently, with one significant difference: as already mentioned, the only barley liquor imported into England was Irish whiskey.

Whisky distilleries sprang up in almost every region of Scotland,

including the Western Isles, but most of all in the Highlands. This mountainous region which covers about half the country was the birthplace of the purest Scottish malts.

The tormented history of whisky was played out by the inhabitants of the Highlands, a history which from the 17th to the 19th centuries involved illegality and smuggling.

Whisky and taxes

Irish whiskey was already the subject of taxation in the 15th century while the first levy on spirits in Scotland was introduced in 1644 under Cromwell. It was abolished after the Restoration.

But the situation changed radically with the Union of the Scottish and English kingdoms in 1707. Parliament quickly extended the existing English tax on malt to Scotland, albeit at half the rate. In spite of this concession Scottish distillers were extremely reluctant to submit to British taxes, and many riots broke out in Edinburgh and Glasgow.

The most immediate consequence of this tax on malt was the proliferation of clandestine distilleries in the Highlands. These mountain regions were ideally suited to the production of illicit whisky because of their inaccessibility and the absence of roads; only the native inhabitants could safely find their way there. But the British malt tax affected other aspects of whisky distillation. To reduce production costs the law-abiding whisky distillers had to reduce the proportion of malted barley they used, replacing it with unmalted cereals. For this reason the belief arose in the 18th century that only illegally produced whisky was the genuine, original Scotch whisky. This had serious consequences for the lawful distilleries, which inevitably found it much harder to sell their legitimate product.

In other words, Scotland experienced what had already happened much earlier in Ireland. There too clandestine distilleries had proliferated, but a clear distinction was quickly made between legitimately distilled and illicit whiskey. The former was known as "parliament" while the latter was called "poteen". The word poteen was derived from the pot still,

the name of the directly-fired still or retort in which Irish whiskey was – and is – distilled.

Naturally, the Irish too were convinced that poteen was better than parliament, particularly because the revenue from it did not enrich the coffers of the English Treasury.

The Highlands and
the clandestine distilleries

As far as Scottish whisky is concerned the 18th century was the period of the clandestine distilleries, which sprang up almost everywhere in the Highlands. Although whisky was also produced in the Lowlands (the less mountainous southern part of Scotland), it was in the Highlands that the most violent conflicts between the distillers and the Treasury took place. The distillers operated in secluded valleys and slopes deep in the mountains. All that was needed was a hole in the ground and a makeshift roof made from tree branches. The stills had a limited capacity, usually between 20 and 50 gallons (roughly 90 to 225 litres). But clandestine distilleries also existed outside the Highlands, in the Lowlands and in Edinburgh. In 1777 there were only eight legal distilleries in Edinburgh but well over four hundred illegal ones.

Excise checks during the first part of the century were actually quite lax, so that the phenomenon of clandestine distilleries which had been developing for centuries was hardly affected while they moved ever closer towards illegality.

In the Highlands, whisky had already virtually become a national drink appreciated by all, with no

distinction of rank or social class. But this was not the case in the Lowlands, where whisky was the preserve of the upper classes, and it was only after the industrial revolution that it became a democratic drink. As Robert Burns said in his famous verse, "Freedom and whisky go together!" The malt distillate became the great social leveller, an escape for the workers and the lower classes in general.

Whisky played a part in everyone's life and it customarily marked important events in life's passage; it might be said that it had a ritual meaning. It was, for instance, the traditional drink at funerals, as it still is in Scotland today. Women too drank whisky, some even starting in the morning, and one of the most popular drinks was toddy, made with whisky, hot water and sugar. Babies were often given a teaspoonful of whisky and men working in the woods would habitually fortify themselves with whisky.

The clandestine distilleries continued to prosper and the situation became no different with the turn of the century. *The Memoirs of a Highland Lady*, written by Elizabeth Grant in the first half of the 19th century, contains this passage: "Balfron was a village where the law was completely ignored. There was a cotton mill and the people who worked there were among the finest in the area. What discredited the region was clandestine distillation. The men would go to the inaccessible forests and valleys of the

Campsie Hills and there distil whisky, which their wives would go and sell at a high price in Glasgow, hiding it in flat containers tied round their waist, forming a kind of corset".

At the end of the 18th century Parliament had imposed new taxes on whisky distilling and this naturally led to a further increase in the number of clandestine distilleries. In 1784, the British Parliament responded to strong protests from the legitimate distillers in the Lowlands and the English gin distillers, who had to pay heavier taxes than their colleagues in the Highlands, by passing the Wash Act. "Wash" is the name given to the fermented wort drained from the mash, the liquid which is subsequently distilled. The 1784 tax made a clear distinction between Scotland's two great whisky producing regions, the Highlands and the Lowlands. In the Lowlands the duty was based on the quantity of wash produced, assuming that 100 gallons (450 litres) of wash would produce 20 gallons (90 litres) of spirit. Each Lowlands distillery had to pay a levy of five pence (2 new pence) on each gallon (4.5 litres) of wash. In the Highlands, on the other hand, it was the individual stills which were taxed, at the rate of twenty shillings (£1) for each gallon of whisky which they could produce.

The law aimed above all to reduce the size of the stills in the Highlands, and therefore their capacity, in order to be able to estimate as accurately as possible the amount of whisky that would be produced. But the High-landers immediately found a way round this by reducing distillation times and thus increasing the production of whisky.

Two years later a new law was passed which increased the levy on Scottish stills and at the same time taxed whisky imported into England, but the increasingly strict legislation only led to an increase in the clandestine selling of whisky, which reached the English markets via the Lowlands.

In 1798 John Stein told the distilleries' commission: "There are thousands of people involved in the distillation of spirits. It is not limited to large cities or authorised producers, but it is scattered all over the country, including all the islands, from the Orkneys to Jura. Among the whisky producers there are many who cannot do anything else, there are some who claim they produce the best whisky but can neither read nor write, and there are others who make whisky in certain parts of the country where the use of the plough is unknown and where the face of an excise agent has never been seen. In these circumstances it is impossible to have exact details of the situation: in order to achieve this one would literally have to make enquiries all over the forests and mountains".

In order to get round this situation,

the English Government offered a reward of £5 to anyone giving information about clandestine distilleries. Naturally the Highlanders were also able to turn this to their advantage, managing to collect the reward without harming the clandestine distillers. In fact, every time they needed to replace the coil of the still – which was the most expensive part of the distilling equipment – they went to the Excise agents claiming they had discovered an illicit distillery. But when the agents arrived there, all they found were a few useless pieces of equipment which had been left behind deliberately after the rest of the equipment had been dismantled and transferred somewhere else. The £5 reward was then used to buy a new coil.

Finally, in 1823, a new law was passed which completely changed things, by succeeding in converting to legality all those who for generations had been involved in clandestine distillation. This was the result of the revolutionary content of the new law, which had been drafted by Alexander, Duke of Gordon. The Duke started from the premise that it would be impossible to eradicate a custom which was so deeply rooted in the soul of the Highlanders. Therefore, what was needed was not repression but an incentive to attract clandestine distillers to legality. The new law imposed a licence duty of £10 on each still with a capacity of 40 gallons (90 litres) or more, and a levy of two shillings and three pence (11.5 new pence) on each gallon (4.5 litres) of spirit produced. The effects of the new law were dramatic. The number of clandestine distilleries dwindled from at least 14,000 in 1823 to 692 in 1834, 177 in 1844, 73 in 1854, 19 in 1867 and 6 in 1874. The great era of clandestine distilleries and illicit whisky was thus brought to an end.

Coffey's revolution

So it was that the 19th century saw the gradual end of clandestine distilleries and their return to the fold of legitimacy. But in the same period the history of whisky was marked by a much more important event which determined the whole of its subsequent development: a revolutionary invention which shook the world of malt distillation to the core and defined the respective destinies of Scotch whisky and Irish whiskey.

Once again it was an Irishman, the engineer Aeneas Coffey, who discovered what could be described as the keystone to whisky production. Coffey was inspector-general of Excise dealing with spirits in Britain, and having spent his working life inspecting distilleries, he designed and patented a new type of still which was named after him. Coffey first proposed his invention to the distillers in Ireland, but they were extremely loth to abandon the traditional type of still they had been using for centuries. The Scottish distillers proved much more far-sighted and they decided to experiment with this new kind of still.

The operation of the pot still, the traditional directly fired still which until then had been used in all Irish and Scottish distilleries will be described later. For the moment it is sufficient to say that Coffey's "patent" still had many advantages over the traditional pot still. Most importantly it could work without interruption, so that more whisky could be produced in a shorter time. In addition, Coffey's still had been designed to produce a distillate made from a blend of malted barley, unmalted barley and other cereals such as maize. The whisky produced in this new still therefore no longer had the peaty aroma which had always distinguished Scottish whisky. The spirit produced in Coffey's still had a harsher taste, much like that of pure alcohol, and it was therefore not easy to market in its natural state. But the whisky distilled using the Coffey system was perfect for blending with the malts produced in the Highlands. It reduced their strong peat aroma, making it an "easier" drink, and one therefore better suited to the English and European markets.

The first blended whisky, that is, the first whisky made from a blend of pure malt whisky and spirit distilled using the Coffey system, appeared in 1850 in Edinburgh. There Andrew Usher, a wine and spirit merchant, began to experiment with mixing the two types, and the result was an immediate success. Until then the English had always preferred Irish whiskey to Scotch, partly because it did not have the smoky peat flavour, and also because the method of distillation made it less harsh; today the Irish continue to distil the wash three times, while the Scots only distil it twice. From 1850 onwards, blended whisky became increasingly popular because of its agreeable qualities.

But this was a disaster for the Irish distillers, who could not compete with the lower price of Scotch; inevitably Irish whiskey was more expensive because it was produced entirely by the traditional method using the pot still over direct heat. It was the end of a centuries-long supremacy.

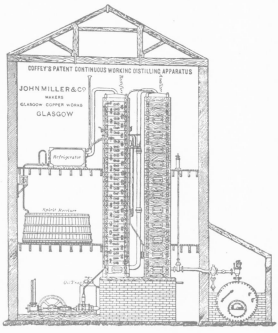

COFFEY'S PATENT CONTINUOUS WORKING DISTILLING APPARATUS

JOHN MILLER & Cº
MAKERS
GLASGOW COPPER WORKS
GLASGOW

Refrigerator

Spirit Receiver

Oil Trap

From the Scottish point of view, this was the start of the remarkable spread of Scotch whisky to every corner of the globe, where it was universally appreciated and respected, and, as will later become apparent, also much imitated or "copied". The legend of Scotch whisky was born.

31

*Scotch whisky from the
19th to the 20th centuries*

But there was another factor which
contributed to the great success of
Scotch whisky throughout the world,
this time unconnected with the Scottish method of distillation.

During the second half of the 19th
century, the phylloxera louse attacked
and destroyed almost all the vines in
France, thus drastically reducing the
production of wine, and therefore of
brandy. The consequent shortage of
what was the most popular spirit in
England and Europe at the end of the
19th century, forced the English, and
then the Europeans, to turn to whisky.

Cognac was a very fashionable
drink at the time, as Winston

Churchill recorded when he wrote: "It is very probable that my father never drank whisky except when he was shooting on the moors or in some other very cold spot. His was the era of brandy and soda". But then it was the turn of whisky and soda, which became the fashionable drink of the British upper classes.

There remained only one problem still to be resolved, and that was whether blended whisky could be called "Scotch whisky", since it was so different from the traditional

Scotch malt whisky from the Highlands. Naturally this issue was raised by the distillers of traditional whisky, who continued to make single malt

whisky and sell it as such. To resolve the question, the English government set up a Commission of experts to weigh up the merits of the case. The Commission gave its verdict in 1909, defining whisky as "a spirit obtained by the distillation of a mixture of cereals saccharified by the action of enzymes of malt". In practice this meant that whisky could be called Scotch whisky whether it was made from a single malt in a still over direct heat, or from cereals using the Coffey system, or from a blend of both. The commission also decided that it was not necessary for the label to specify the kinds of distillates used in the blending or the relative percentages. Only in 1915 was a law passed requiring ageing for at least three years.

Whisky crosses the Atlantic

Long before Scotch whisky began its long, glorious voyage across the seas, straight spirits made from cereals had already crossed the Atlantic and reached the New World. Irish and Scottish settlers who had left their country to find their fortune in the lush prairies of America brought their customs and traditions with them, and whisky was undoubtedly one of the settlers' most deeply rooted traditions.

From the 17th century, the territory which was later to become the United States was colonised by the French and the British, the latter settling mainly in what are now the states of New England, Maryland, Carolina, Georgia, Virginia, Kentucky and Pennsylvania. Meanwhile, the English founded Nova Scotia in Canada in 1604 and moved steadily towards the interior, conquering Quebec and Ontario which had been colonised by the French. Until the end of the 17th century rum had been the national drink of the English settlers, but this changed with the arrival of the Irish and Scottish emigrants who started distilling whisky. In the space of a century this became the national drink, at least in the states where it was produced.

Many experts believe that the first distilleries were founded as early as the beginning of the 18th century, and this is probably true. However, there are no precise and consistent references to these early distilleries until 1770–80. On the other hand, it is known for certain that in the mid-18th century the county of Cumberland in Pennsylvania boasted at least one distillery along the Juniata river. Thereafter distilleries sprang up almost everywhere in the states colonised by the British, especially in the then county of Kentucky, in West Virginia.

In the American War of Independence the French joined forces with those who were rebelling against the London government, and after their victory many towns and counties adopted French names as a sign of gratitude. So it was that a part of the county of Kentucky, which was repeatedly divided, was named Bourbon in honour of the French royal family.

In 1792 Kentucky became an independent state, and Bourbon has remained one of its counties. Here, production of whiskey (the Americans adopted the Irish spelling) was already well-established and widespread. It is said that Thomas Jefferson, governor of Virginia and future president of the United States, had encouraged settlers to come and establish themselves in Virginia by offering them sixty acres of land to cultivate maize. The harvest of maize was so large that no family could use it all as food and therefore many started to distil it, exactly as they had done in Ireland and Scotland

with barley. In the early days of its existence as an independent state, whiskey often replaced money and was used as barter. The town of Maysville in the county of Bourbon was used as a port on the Ohio river, and it was here that most of the whiskey produced in the state left for various destinations.

Although it might appear strange, the county of Bourbon was never a very important centre of distillation and nowadays no whiskey is produced there at all, partly because of the very strict anti-alcohol laws. The most important centre of whiskey production was Louisville and today, together with Bardstown and Frankfort, the capital of Kentucky, it continues to play a leading role in the production of whiskey in the United States.

According to some historians, it

was the Reverend Elijah Craig, the Baptist pastor who founded Georgetown, who first produced Bourbon in 1789. In actual fact it is more likely that he only codified production techniques and that whiskey had already been produced there for years.

Naturally, American whiskey was not only produced in Kentucky. It was also made in Maryland, Pennsylvania, Virginia and Tennessee. In Virginia one of the most important producers was George Washington who continued to produce whiskey until 1789, being elected president in 1794.

A little later, another American President was able to boast of his past as a distiller, Abraham Lincoln, a native of Kentucky.

Each state produced whiskey using different methods, and the difference between the various whiskies depended mainly on which cereals were used in the blend and the proportions.

In Canada, too, whisky distilling had become well established (unlike their neighbours the Canadians adopted the Scottish spelling). In 1763 the province of Ontario came under English rule, and it was there that the first distilleries appeared at the end of the 18th century, concentrated mainly round the town of Kingston, between Toronto and Ottawa. As in the United States, the production of whisky in Canada started as a family craft activity but it soon became an important industry employing many people.

The province of Ontario has many waterways, and distilleries were built along the shores of Lake Erie and Lake Ontario, extending northward along the St Lawrence river, and even spreading into the territory of Quebec. By 1840 there were already two hundred whisky distilleries in Canada. Today, the production of Canadian whisky has spread as far west as the Pacific coast of in British Columbia, but the main centre of whisky production remains the region between

Ontario and Quebec, between the cities of Windsor in the south and Montreal in the north.

Wars and Prohibition

The period including the two World Wars and the time of Prohibition America had serious consequences on world markets for both whisky and whiskey. In most cases distilleries were requisitioned to produce industrial alcohol, but exports were to some extent safeguarded since they already played an important part in the nation's finances. Often it was also necessary to reduce the supply of cereals available for distillation in order to avoid food shortages.

In 1915 the production of whisky was officially restricted in Britain and completely stopped two years later. When normal conditions returned at the end of the war, many small distilleries could not resume business having been hit so hard by this enforced closure, and many others joined forces to survive. In the meantime, taxes on whisky continued to increase, creating serious problems on the market.

The outbreak of the Second World War certainly did not help world markets and whisky suffered along with many other exports. In 1939 the British Ministry of Food decided to

stop all whisky distillation, and it was only in 1944 that manufacturers were allowed to produce a small amount of whisky exclusively for export. Rationing was introduced in 1940, since, although whisky production had been stopped, there was still an ample supply ageing in casks. Whisky rationing ended in 1954 but it was only in the late 1950s that enough was produced to satisfy the demand.

To understand the importance of whisky exports in the English economy after the War, one has only to read a note written by Winston Churchill in 1945. "There is no reason to reduce the amount of barley intended for whisky production. Whisky takes years to mature and it is a priceless export because of all the dollars it brings into the country. Taking into account all our other problems regarding export, it would be extremely foolish not to try and preserve this traditional, prestigious flagship of our economy."

Before the outbreak of the Second World War, international markets for whisky and whiskey were greatly complicated by the consequences of Prohibition in America. In fact, during the Prohibition years Scotch whisky was imported secretly from Canada. During the First World War all Canadian distilleries had been requisitioned for the production of industrial alcohol. Scotch whisky was therefore imported from Britain to be blended with alcohol of uncertain origin before being smuggled into the United States.

Throughout the whole of the Prohibition period (1919–34) the United States continued to be an important market for Canadian whisky, partly because Canada could produce whisky again after the War, although only for export. It was plain that Canadian whisky was destined for the adjacent American market, but the government turned a blind eye because the returns from this clandestine commerce were so enormous.

While some people amassed huge fortunes, there were others who were unable to escape from the downward spiral created by the – at least theoretically – "dry" policy of the United States. This was the case with two particular whiskies (both with an "e" this time): Irish whiskey and Pennsylvania whiskey.

Irish whiskey had already suffered a severe blow when Coffey's still was introduced and blended whisky began appearing on the market. Exports dwindled during the first two decades of the 20th century, and the situation was not improved by the War, the rationing of cereals and the subsequent ending of all distillation. When Prohibition in the United States was finally ended in 1934, Irish distilleries were unable to meet the demand from the American continent, which increasingly turned to Scotland for its whisky. It was only in the 1960s that Irish whiskey succeeded in reconquering some of its former international markets as a result of the merger of the largest distilleries and some high-powered advertising campaigns. Its popularity is still increasing.

But the situation was different in the case of Pennsylvania whiskey, known as rye after the main cereal used in its production (at least 51 per cent). During Prohibition, Scotch whisky flavoured with rye had been imported into the United States from Canada and this had greatly confused consumers. The 1950s marked the end of the great Pennsylvania rye, but since the 1980s this rye-flavoured whisky with its complex aroma and "difficult" taste appears to have found some new markets.

Whisky with almond eyes

At the beginning of the century, whisky distilled in Scotland found another very interesting market: Japan. Scotch whisky soon came to be seen as an exotic, elitist drink in Japan, so that as early as the 1920s Japan started to produce its own. The first distillery was built in 1923 in the Yamazaki valley, near Kyoto. But Japanese whisky only really took off after the Second World War.

The early Japanese distillers were greatly influenced by Scotch whisky. In fact, the Japanese spirit can be seen as a direct descendant of the whisky from the Highlands. Japan has a great number of springs with crystal clear water very like those in Scotland and it also has peat, especially in the northern isle of Hokkaido. As a result

44

the first Japanese whisky had a strong peaty flavour and was not unlike those produced in Scotland. But as time went by peat was used less and less. In fact, the Japanese were now aiming to produce their own national whisky, rather than directly copy Scotch whisky, which today is still considered a very special drink, the founder spirit. The Japanese home market wanted a whisky with a lighter flavour, in other words less peaty. As a result the production of Japanese whisky doubled in the 1970s, and it increased by a further 50 per cent in the 1980s.

Another decisive factor in the growth of Japanese whisky on the home market was the appearance of the "whisky bar", created by the distillers themselves. Whisky is the only drink served in these whisky bars, and they have another very unusual feature. Customers buy a whole bottle of whisky which is kept in a personal locker. This is used whenever the customer comes in until the bottle is finished. The Japanese have a culture of generous hospitality, and in this way they are able to offer their "own" whisky to their friends as if they were at home.

Today, Japan is the second largest producer of whisky in the world after the United States. It also boasts the world's largest malt whisky distillery

– Hakushu – producing more than 55 million bottles a year. Although the Japanese consider their own whisky a national drink for the home market, it is increasingly exported and Japanese whisky is now making an appearance on almost all international markets.

WHISKY
ALL OVER THE WORLD

SCOTCH WHISKY

The three basic elements – The malt whisky produced in the various regions of Scotland is still made using the same methods as in the 18th and 19th centuries, although the process has naturally been improved and the equipment perfected. The main difference from the past is the way in which malt whisky is now used: today most of it becomes part of blended whisky and only a small amount is put on the market in its "pure" state.

The fundamental elements used in the manufacture of malt whisky are barley, water and peat. As far as the barley is concerned, in the past this was all grown in Scotland, but in more recent times some began to be imported. Today, it is estimated that only 42 per cent of the cereals used in making whisky is cultivated in Scotland, 35 per cent comes from England and the rest from Canada and Australia. In practice the source of the barley does not affect the finished product. What really gives whisky its particular character is the water.

Scotland is a land rich in water, known for its purity and absence of mineral salts. Every distillery has its own stream or river whose water is used to manufacture the whisky. This is why the malt whisky produced by each distillery is different from that of the other distillers. According to some experts, the best water for making whisky is that "which comes out of granite through peat", while others hold that it is better that it should "come out of peat through granite".

The second distinctive element of each malt whisky is the way peat is used during the process of drying the malt. As well as the intrinsic characteristics of the water which are naturally passed on to the whisky, the peat itself is used differently depending on the kind of product the maker aims to achieve. In this case it is man's intervention which determines the nature of the final product, its more or less "smoky" flavour in particular.

Now it is time to look in greater detail at the various stages in the process of making malt whisky.

Malting – Malting is the process of germinating cereals (normally barley) under special conditions to encourage the development of an enzyme system which makes fermentation possible. Ungerminated cereals do not produce the sugar known as maltose. That is why a certain amount of malted barley must be used in the manufacture of whisky.

The barley is threshed immediately after the harvest, in September to October, and then sold to the distilleries. It is essential that the grain is ripe and dry, since it would otherwise go mouldy. Before being used the grain is winnowed and dried in special ovens or in silos in which hot air is circulated. Once the barley has dried sufficiently it is placed in large

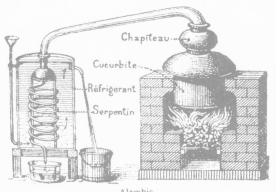

Alambic.

vats to which water is added to encourage germination. This initial process of maceration may last from 48 to 70 hours depending on the atmospheric conditions. All the surplus water is removed and the barley is then moved to the actual malting "floor". Here, the grain is spread out over a stone, cement or tile surface, to a depth of 60–90 cm (24–36 in). The barley germinates on this surface, absorbing oxygen and releasing carbon dioxide. In the course of doing this it produces a large amount of heat. The temperature is higher in the bottom layers, and to even it out and maintain it at 15°C (59°F), the grain is thrown into the air and turned over with shovels once or twice a day. This turning of the grain is also helpful in preventing the sprouting barley from becoming entangled. The malt is no longer turned over by hand in all distilleries; there are mechanical ways of achieving the same result such as Saladin's box and the Wanderhaufen method, which do the job perfectly without difficulty.

The barley remains in the maltings for a period of about eight to fourteen days, depending on whether the grain is turned over mechanically or by hand. When the barley sprouts have reached a length equal to five eighths of that of the grain of barley, it is ready for the next phase, the drying process.

At this point the thickness of the layer of barley will have reduced considerably from its original depth of 60 cm (2 ft). The grains will have softened and acquired a chalky appearance. The writer David Daiches remembers being told by an old man who had worked all his life in a distillery that the barley was ready when "you could write your name on the wall with a grain".

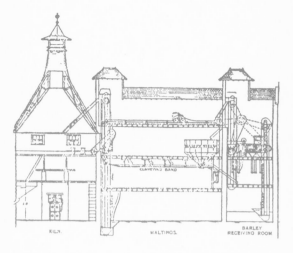

KILN.　　　MALTINGS.　　　BARLEY RECEIVING ROOM

Now called "green malt", the barley next goes into the drying ovens where it is placed on a metal grid at a height of 30–90 cm (12–36in) above the ground. The peat fire is then lit under the grid so that its characteristic aroma permeates the green malt.

Today very few distilleries use exclusively peat as fuel. Most of them now resort mainly to coke or anthracite, using peat only at the beginning of the drying process so that the malt can absorb some of its fragrance. But the most modern and quickest drying systems use hot air with a peaty fragrance which is circulated through the ovens by means of fans. With this type of system 24 hours are enough to dry the green malt thoroughly, while conferring on it the characteristic "smoky" flavour.

Some distilleries have moved even further away from tradition and no

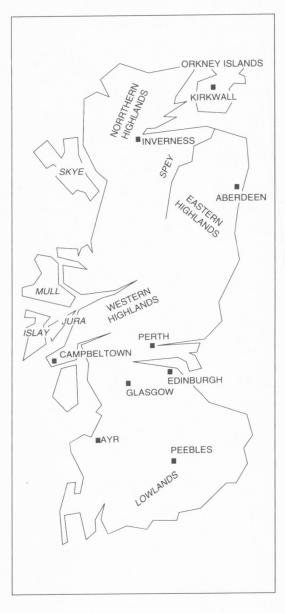

longer perform these tasks themselves; they buy malt which has
already been dried and peat-
flavoured directly from the malting

54

house. In general, it may be said that the most "traditional" distilleries are those on the island of Islay, which carry out the malting themselves and use only peat for drying the malt.

Mashing – Once the drying phase is completed a special machine is used to remove all the barley germs or shoots. Once cleaned, the grains are then ground in a mill. The resulting "flour" (which must not be too fine) is then mixed with warm water and put in a container called a mash-tun. The warm water reactivates the enzyme action, converting the starch in the grains of barley into maltose and other fermentable sugars. Water is added several times to the mash-tun, raising its temperature gradually to 80°C (176°F) from its initial 60–68°C (140–154°F). The mash is

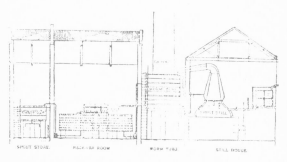

SPIRIT STORE. RECEIVER ROOM WORM TUBS STILL HOUSE

continually churned by a mixing device consisting of special revolving rakes or knives. The liquid must from the first two extractions of the malt, known as the "wort", is then drained off through the bottom of the mash-tun into a vessel called an "underback" which is placed underneath it. From there the wort is conveyed to the fermentation vats. The liquid from the third and the fourth extractions cannot really be called "malt must" since it is much less concentrated. It is therefore recycled and

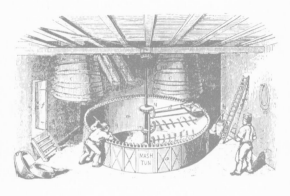

poured back into the next lot of malt to be mashed. The wort is a warm, semi-transparent, sticky liquid with a sweetish taste.

Fermentation – Before going into the fermentation vats, the must is cooled down to a temperature of 20–27°C (68–81°F). This operation is necessary because the excessive heat would cause the maltose to decompose, as well as destroying the yeast which is to be used in the next phase. The fermentation vats range in capacity from

4,500 to 60,000 litres (1,000 to 13,000 gallons), depending on the importance of the distillery. Traditionally, the fermentation vats are always made of wood (larch or pine), but today many distilleries prefer to use stainless steel vats like those used for wine. The vats are filled only to three quarters of their capacity because the wort ferments violently and it could "boil over".

It is at this moment that a carefully measured amount of yeast is added to the wort. This triggers a tumultuous and even noisy reaction: the yeast acts on the sugars, transforming them into alcohol and carbon dioxide. This gas causes the liquid to seethe, generating quantities of foam and bubbles. The fermentation phase is a very delicate one and it is carefully watched. In the past workers would check the fermentation vats constantly, stirring the mass of foaming liquid to prevent excessive formation of foam. This operation has also been mechanised, but human supervision is still needed to ensure that everything proceeds as it should.

In the space of 36 to 48 hours all the maltose is transformed into dextrose, or in other words glucose, which in turn is converted into alcohol and carbon dioxide by the action of the yeast. The resulting liquid is clear and consists of water, yeast and about

5 per cent alcohol. This fermented wort which has not yet been distilled is known as *wash*.

Distillation – The process of distillation consists of bringing the liquid to a temperature where the alcohol (but not the water) boils and becomes vapour, which is then cooled down to obtain a pure liquid as a condensate.

In Scotland the wash is distilled twice in two copper stills of different

sizes. In the first, known as the "wash still", the fermented must evaporates and rises through the neck of the still; it then passes through a coil immersed in a container filled with cold water. There it is condensed and converted back to liquid. This first distillate is put in a container known as "tank for low wines". The Scots use the term "low wines" for the result of this first distillation, a reference to the fact that the spirit obtained at this stage is still impure.

From the " low wines tank" the liquid then passes directly to the second still, which is the same shape as the first but smaller. The spirit produced after the second distillation is then collected in a spirit safe, a kind of well-sealed brass tank with glass sides to which only excise officials have the key. Using special taps, the still man (the person in charge of distillation) can transfer a sample of the spirit into a vessel containing a hydrometer

which measures the specific gravity of the liquid, from which its alcoholic content can be calculated. This may be adjusted by dilution with distilled water.

These operations are carried out to check whether the spirit obtained after the second distillation can be defined as whisky or not. The still man is the most important person in the distillery because he is responsible for the successful outcome of the whole operation. He must decide whether the liquor in the safe can be transferred to the spirit receiver (the container to hold the distillate for the next stage), or whether it should be returned to the low wines container to be distilled again. The first and last "streams" of the distillate – known respectively as the "foreshot" and "feints" – must be removed and distilled again because they are full of impurities.

It is therefore up to the still man to decide what parts of the distillation will become whisky, in other words when the foreshot ends and when the feints start. Any errors made by the still man at this point will not be discovered for several years, when the whisky has completely matured in the barrel, and by then it is impossible to rectify the damage.

Unlike wort from malt, the various cereal worts are distilled in the Coffey or column-still. This operates continuously and effectively consists of two distillation columns, the first of which acts as a "rectifier" for purification and the second as a selector.

Once distillation is completed the whisky is finally put into barrels to mature. At this stage the whisky is still colourless and it has an alcoholic strength of 65–70°, which is reduced to 60° by the addition of spring water.

Maturation – As already mentioned, British law requires a minimum of three years of maturation for both Scottish whisky and Irish whiskey. But most malt whisky on the market has been matured for at least five years in wood. This process takes place in barrels of various sizes. Naturally, the larger the container the slower the process of maturation, because of the proportionately smaller area of contact with the wood which influences the exchange between the wood and the whisky.

The traditional barrels used for mature whisky are made of oak with a capacity of 500 litres (110 gallons), which have already been used tor ageing sherry. It is the wood impregnated with sherry which gives whisky its golden colour as well as a particular aroma. If the sherry aged in the barrel was pale, the whisky will take on a very light golden colour, while if, on the other hand, the barrel was used for a darker sherry the whisky will acquire a more amber colour with a fuller aroma.

However, the very large quantities of Scottish whisky that are produced have made it impossible to find enough sherry barrels for this purpose. Distillers have therefore been obliged to re-use staves from old whisky barrels which are reassembled by master coopers. It has also been necessary to look for other practical alternatives. One of the commonest solutions is the use of barrels in which Bourbon has matured, because according to American law these can only been used once. Another alternative is to use barrels of new wood impregnated with *paxarete*, a substance used in Jerez to colour sherry and obtained from heated grape juice.

During the process of maturation the volume of whisky is to some extent reduced by evaporation. The Scots describe this very poetically as

"the angels' share". It is a phenomenon which is most noticeable in small barrels. So, although the process of maturation is slower in large barrels, more whisky is lost through evaporation in small barrels.

It is usually said that whisky in barrel improves with age. However, after about fifteen years the continued storage of whisky in wood becomes risky, in that it may become permeated with unpleasant "barrel taint".

After maturing, malt whisky is nearly ready to be put on the market. But before it is bottled more spring water must be added to reduce its alcoholic strength to the limits imposed in the various countries.

Some 95 per cent of the malt whisky produced in the 116 distilleries in Scotland is destined for blending, only the remaining 5 per cent being sold as single malt whisky. The definition of a single malt is a whisky from a single distillery. There are also whiskies which are made from the malts of various distilleries. The whisky is then called "vatted malt", and it is produced by blending malt whiskies only.

Vatted malt is sometimes produced to represent a particular zone of production, but it is more often designed to balance out the different characteristics of single malts. For instance, one well-known vatted whisky is a blend of four different malts: "one for perfume, one for taste, one for body and the fourth for its ability to blend all four into a harmonious, mellow drink".

Blending – As already mentioned, most of the malt whisky produced in Scotland is intended for blending. This blending takes place in large, modern distilleries, most of which are situated around Glasgow and Edinburgh.

Many people describe blending as an art, and indeed human skills here play a major part by selecting the malts to be included in the mixture and determining the percentage of each ingredient in the blend. A blended whisky is not produced by simply mixing a malt and a cereal spirit, but by "marrying" a number of malt whiskies, from fifteen to as many as forty, with one or more cereal-based whiskies.

The selection of malts, their number and their proportions all depend on the "nose" of the master blender who is in charge of blending. It takes years of practice to develop a master blender's "nose", and they themselves are often sons of master blenders. There are no books or classes teaching the art of blending, and distilleries are extremely secretive about their formulas. That is why the blender is often a blender's son, who is likely to have been initiated into the art of blending from a tender age.

Naturally, the price of blended whisky depends in the first place on how much malt it contains. Generally speaking, a good blended whisky should contain at least 50 per cent malt whisky. Much Scotch whisky on the market only contains 40 per cent of malt, and in some cases as little as 10 per cent. National tastes vary, and the Americans prefer "light" Scotch whisky, while Italians favour a stronger, more pronounced taste, so much so that Italy is now the world's largest importer of single malts.

The blending process is a relatively simple operation. When all the various whiskies selected by the blender arrive at the distillery, they are carried through stainless steel channels into a large vat where they are blended either by traditional, mechanical means or by the introduction of compressed air. At this stage a small quantity of sherry or caramel may be added to give more colour to the whisky. The addition of caramel has the further purpose of keeping the colour of the blend similar from year to year, as expected by consumers who are used to a particular type of product.

From the vat the blended whisky is put into oak barrels where it is left to "rest" for at least six months. Some distilleries blend only the malt whiskies in the vat, adding the grain spirit at the moment it is bottled. It appears that this produces a more mellow blend.

Where an age is mentioned on the label of a bottle of Scotch, this refers to the youngest malt that has been used in the blend.

As a curiosity, it should here be mentioned that there is a whisky available in Britain containing no malt whisky; it is produced exclusively from cereals and bottled by a distillery in Fife, in the Lowlands. There are also at least three other whiskies

marketed as single grain whiskies which are bottled by merchants.

How to recognise Scottish whisky – Historically, there are four Scottish whisky regions: the Lowlands, Campbeltown, Islay and the Highlands. Speaking generally and referring only to the single malts, it may be said that malt whiskies from the Lowlands are lighter in taste, while those from Islay are usually stronger.

In the past the Lowland malts used to be overlooked because they were believed to be inferior to those from the Highlands. In addition, the malts from the Highlands benefited from a long, romantic history of illegal distillers and smugglers, which greatly contributed to their fascination and fame throughout the world. But in fact the whiskies from the Lowlands merit attention because they have distinct personalities and well-defined characteristics. While it is true that the aroma is less peaty, it is also sweeter and fruitier.

In some ways the Lowland malts are an excellent introduction for beginners to the world of malt whisky. Fortunately, the renewed success of single malt whiskies in general since the 1970s has also benefited the malts made by the ten distilleries situated in the Lowlands.

Campbeltown, a small town on the Mull of Kintyre (the subject of Paul McCartney's song of the same name), gives its name to the second traditional production zone of Scotch whisky. It is one of the smallest regions with only two distilleries (in the mid-19th century there were about thirty). The Campbeltown malts are distinguished by a discreet peatiness combined with a hint of brackishness reflecting its closeness to the sea. The barrels in which the whisky is aged are actually impregnated with brine, thus giving the whisky its pungent, salty aroma which is described by connoisseurs as "sea mist".

Not surprisingly, the Highlands are the largest production region of single malts with over ninety-six distilleries. The region stretches northwards from an imaginary line between Dundee in the east and Greenock in the west, and includes the archipelagoes of the Orkneys and the Hebrides, but excluding the Isle of Islay which is a region in its own right as far as whisky is concerned. Seen as a whole, the malts from the Highlands are full-bodied, robust and dry, with a definite characteristic smoky aroma which makes them quite unmistakable and unique. But of course in such a vast region there bound to be a wide range of flavours and bouquets.

The Highlands are customarily divided into several sub-regions. The western Highlands include the Isles of

Skye, Mull and Jura, while the northern Highlands include the Isle of Kirkwall in the Orkneys. The Speyside region between Inverness and Aberdeen in the northeast is crossed by the River Spey where most Scottish distilleries are situated. The eastern Highlands region extends south of Aberdeen, and finally there is the Midlands region between the Highlands and Lowlands.

It is not easy to describe the differences between the whiskies of the various sub-regions of the Highlands. In general and without claiming to be exhaustive, it can be said that the malts of the northern Highlands and the Isle of Kirkwall have a slightly spicy flavour, reminiscent of heather. Those of the eastern Highlands have a much more complex aroma with a distinctive peatiness, beautifully combined with fruity, aromatic fragrances. The malts of Speyside, which in fact forms part of eastern Scotland, have more or less similar characteristics, but in addition they have a particular soft mellowness which distinguishes them from the other eastern malts. The three western isles each have their own distilleries, Skye undoubtedly producing the most typical of the "island whiskies", very strong and intense with a smoky aroma. The malts of Mull and Jura are lighter and softer and they are therefore more similar to the malts produced in the western Highlands.

The fourth and last region producing single malt whisky is the Isle of Islay, which has eight distilleries. They produce the most traditional, conservative whiskies of all Scotland. They are very pungent malts because of the twin effects of peat and brine, and their aroma is often described as reminiscent of "seaweed" or "iodine", and sometimes even as "medicinal". The frequent storms which batter the island during the winter months leave salt deposits on the ground so that as

well as penetrating the wooden barrels in which the whisky is left to mature, the "smell of the sea" also impregnates the peat used to dry the grains of barley after maceration.

Aeneas Macdonald once said that "Scottish whiskies are like an orchestra. The malts from Islay are solemn and dusky like the cellos. The malts from the Highlands are the violas, those of the Lowlands are the violins, and the grain whiskies are like the piano, sometimes *fortissimo* and sometimes *pianissimo*". This is indeed a lyrical way of describing various kinds of Scotch and it could only have been said by a Scot. Perhaps this is the best approach to the appreciation of the wonderful world of the malt whiskies of Scotland.

IRISH WHISKEY

The production process – In its production, Irish whiskey undergoes a series of processes which are much the same as those used in making its Scottish cousin. However, there are a few differences which give Irish whiskey a more or less unique, unmistakable personality, which is much appreciated by connoisseurs.

The first difference between Irish whiskey and Scottish whisky lies in the mixture of cereals used. As has already been mentioned, during the 19th century the increased levy on malt forced Irish distillers to use a certain percentage of unmalted barley. This mixture was pleasing to both producers and consumers, so much so that it remained one of the main characteristics of Irish whiskey even after the abolition of the tax.

Another change in the original recipe was introduced more recently. In the first half of the 20th century, Ireland had yielded to Scotland its supremacy in the production and export of whiskey. Indeed, blended Scotch whisky was becoming increasingly popular internationally, especially in the American market which had always shown a preference for lighter spirits. In order to give their whiskey a new image and to make it more "accessible", some Irish distillers began to include some spirit made from mixed cereals (oat, wheat and rye), using continuous column stills. In other words, the Irish decided to adapt to modern tastes while preserving the distinctive, original character of their whiskey.

Indeed for many years whiskey made exclusively from barley continued to be preferred in Ireland itself, while that blended from mixed cereal spirit was destined mainly for export. Today the situation has completely changed and the majority of Irish whiskey is now a blend of spirits made from malted barley, unmalted barley and other cereals. In practice there are differences in the proportions of malt and other spirits used, depending on whether the whiskey is intended for the home market or the international market.

Today there is only one Irish whiskey which boasts malt barley as

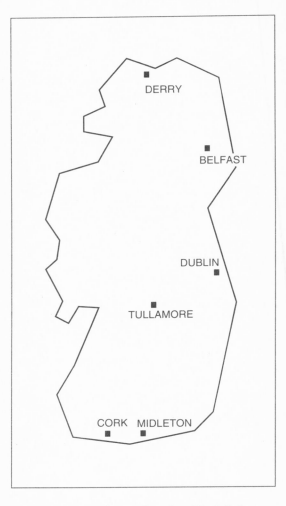

its sole ingredient: Bushmills Malt.

The second significant difference between whiskey and whisky lies in the fact that the Irish do not use peat in the drying process of the already partially germinated barley. Irish distillery ovens are closed and they are usually stoked with coal so that the malt has no hint of a smoky aroma.

The actual process of distillation in

Ireland is also different. First, the Irish stills are larger than the Scottish ones; secondly, the malt wort and barley are distilled three times, rather than twice as is normal in Scotland. This triple distillation is probably necessary because of the inclusion of unmalted barley, which is very robust. The result is a spirit with a rather higher alcoholic strength than its twice-distilled Scottish relative. Irish whiskey therefore has to be diluted with more spring water than Scotch whisky.

The whiskey is now ready to be put into the barrels where it must remain for a minimum of three years. In fact, in Ireland as in Scotland, the process of maturation usually lasts at least five years, during which time the whiskey lies in oak barrels, some of which have previously been used to mature sherry.

The process of maturation can last as long as fifteen years. When completed, the malt and barley whiskey is blended with grain spirit produced from mixed cereals. The Irish call this operation "vatting" rather than blending, but it is a more or less similar process with a number of malts being blended together with one or more cereal-based whiskies. But unlike the Scottish blended whiskies, the vatted Irish whiskies are the result of the marriage of a relatively small number of whiskies produced in a traditional pot-still, and grain whiskey. There are indeed Irish whiskies produced from just one malt and one grain spirit.

How to recognise Irish whiskey – One effect of Prohibition was that the export of whiskey dropped drastically

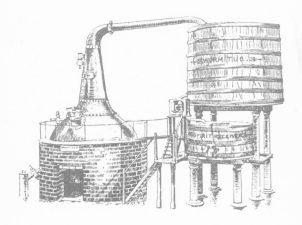

and quite a few distilleries were forced to close down. Between the 1920s and the 1960s Irish whiskey reverted to its status of a "local" product again, in the sense that few people outside Ireland really knew it.

To revive the image of Irish whiskey and its thousand-year old history, four distilleries which had survived the long-term crisis of the Irish whiskey industry merged to form a single group which took the name of the Irish Distillers Group. They set up an enormous single production plant in Midleton, County Cork, in the south of the country. In 1974 they were joined by a distillery from Northern Ireland which enabled the group to relaunch Irish whiskey on the international market.

Today the two distillery centres are Midleton in Eire and Bushmills in

Ulster. The blending (vatting) and bottling take place in Dublin, Cork (Ireland's second largest city) and Tullamore, a small town in the centre of the country which has had a distillery since the 1950s.

The fact that all the Irish distilleries belong to a single group might lead one to believe that all their labels contain a similar product. Nothing could be further from the truth. The large production plant in Midleton is able to produce a dozen whiskies which are all different in their composition and therefore aroma and taste. The differences are due to the different percentages of malt whiskey used, the vatting, and how long the spirit is left to mature in barrels.

Whatever the different blends used in vatting and the variety of maturation periods, all Irish whiskies have one thing in common, which at the same time distinguishes them from Scotch. This is the absence of the smoky or peaty fragrance which enables the sweetness of barley and roundness of malt to come to the fore and be perceived by the nose and mouth. The more traditional whiskies have an ethereal perfume as well as a hint of sherry in the taste.

Whiskey from Northern Ireland is different again, being made by blending several single malt whiskies with one grain whiskey (there is even one brand of single malt whiskey). The malt used in the Bushmills distillery is also briefly treated with peat which explains a certain hint of dryness in its fragrance, although it would be hard to detect an actual smoky aroma.

WHISKEY IN THE UNITED STATES

The many whiskies of the United States – The world of American whiskey is one of vast distilleries with continuous column stills, very different from the traditional pear-shaped pot-stills which occupy the place of honour in the distilleries of the Highlands and Ireland. Another difference is that maize is the supreme cereal, rather than barley. Maize, or corn, is native to North America. It is easy to cultivate with a very short vegetative cycle, allowing alternation with other crops within the same year.

As well as maize, American distillers use rye, oat, wheat and barley. Whiskey in the United States is categorised on the basis of the main cereal in the fermentation mixture. Thus, a whiskey is a *Bourbon* (named after Bourbon county, Kentucky) when maize constitutes at least 51 per cent of the mixture; a *rye* or a *wheat* respectively when either of these is the main ingredient; a *malt* when malted barley is the main ingredient, and *corn* when maize makes up at least 80 per cent of the fermentation mixture.

The various whiskies are divided into three broad categories: *straight*, *light* and *blended*. The first category, straight, includes all the unblended whiskies whose main ingredient may be rye, maize, wheat or barley. The regulations allow a straight whiskey to be removed from the still when its alcoholic strength is no greater than 80° in order to preserve the volatile elements which distinguish its organoleptic profile. Before being bottled this whiskey must be matured in completely new barrels for at least two years.

The category of light whiskey was only recognised in 1972; it was created to satisfy the requirements of an American market increasingly keen on "light" distillates. Any type of cereal may be used to produce a light, but on the whole distillers prefer to use a high percentage of maize. Lights are aged for at least two years but the barrels can be old and they do not have to be charred, unlike those used for straight whiskey.

Although the category of light was created to meet public demand, the commercial success of this whiskey has been less than the distillers expected. Consequently, many lights are now used in the production of blended whiskey.

According to the law, blended whiskey, the third category, must contain at least 20 per cent of straight whiskey. Interestingly, the blends have not been particularly successful with the public either, because they are judged too light by the lovers of straight whiskey and too strong or heavy by those who prefer distillates with a lower alcoholic strength. The 1980s in the United States also saw a renewed interest in distillates with a more "decisive", "defined" taste, so much so that the straights are becoming increasingly popular in the American market.

Bourbon – Bourbon is a straight whiskey in which maize represents at least 51 per cent, with the addition of rye, and sometimes oats as well, to add flavour to the mixture, and malted barley to trigger off the process of fermentation. The label carries the name "Kentucky Bourbon Whiskey", which means that the distillate was produced and aged for at least one year in the State of Kentucky.

With Bourbon, maturation in charred oak barrels is extremely important. The origin of the use of charred oak is uncertain and there are various legends on the subject. According to one of these stories, which may well be true, a distiller had bought a number of barrels which had been used to store fish. In order to get rid of the smell, he decided to char the inside of the barrels, which proved to have surprisingly agreeable results on the whiskey matured in them.

Generally speaking, all the straight whiskies are matured for at least four

years, the label only displaying the age of the product if the period of maturation exceeds four years.

The words "sour mash" on the label indicate that the Bourbon, or any other type of straight whiskey, has been produced by the acid infusion method. This consists of collecting some of the distillation residues from the bottom of the distillation column (known as "backset") and adding them to the grain mash, the yeast mash or even the fermentation tank. Used only in the United States, the purpose of this technique is to ensure continuous fermentation.

How to recognise whiskey from the United States – The states which produce whiskey are, from north to south, Pennsylvania, Maryland, Virginia, Kentucky and Tennessee. It is understandable that in such a large production area the style of the many different whiskies should vary enormously. These differences in style are most of all due to the kind of cereal used as the main ingredient in the fermentation mixture. Rye whiskey, for instance, will have some of the bitterness of rye, with a hint of fruit and spice, and a trace of mint. The rye whiskey states are Pennsylvania, Maryland and Virginia, but it is also produced in Kentucky.

In contrast to rye whiskey, Bourbon has the characteristic sweetness of maize with an aroma of vanilla as a result of being aged in new, charred barrels. It is in fact the very charring of the barrels which increases the exchange between the wood and the whiskey, not only giving it an unmistakable aroma but also an amber colour which in this case has nothing to do with caramel.

Bourbon is undoubtedly the best known American whiskey in the world. It is produced in all the states mentioned apart from Tennessee, whose whiskey represents a category in its own right.

Like Bourbon, the distillate produced in Tennessee is based on a mixture of cereals with a preponderance of maize. But while other whiskies are filtered just before they are bottled, the whiskey produced in Tennessee undergoes a long process of filtration before being put in barrels to mature.

The spirit is filtered through charcoal immediately after it is distilled, so that it is "cleaner" when put in the barrels. It has not yet been established if the use of charcoal "removes" or "adds" something to the aroma, but there is no doubt that Tennessee whiskey is very different from all the other whiskies produced in the United States. The final result is a mellow distillate with a particularly dry, clean taste.

CANADIAN WHISKY

The Canadian "style" – It has already been described how the illegal import of Canadian whisky into the United States during Prohibition created considerable confusion among the regular consumers of Pennsylvania rye whiskey.

The Canadians also used rye as a main ingredient when they first started producing whisky, and they simply called their distillate rye. However, at the end of the 19th century, or to be precise in 1884, Hiram Walker launched his Canadian Club whisky. This was to have a crucial impact on the Canadian spirit which developed a style of its own, the result of a marriage between rye whisky and other grain-based whiskies. Canadian rye was no longer a straight rye like that produced in the United States, yet it continues to be called rye both in the common language and on the label.

Today maize, rye, barley and even small quantities of wheat are used in

producing Canadian whisky. The Canadian style is the result of blending more than one rye whisky with distillates of various cereals, and rather large amounts of neutral alcohol. Often the neutral alcohol used in blending is produced from rye but rectified to such a degree that it has become an almost odourless, tasteless spirit.

For blending, the Canadians also produce a whisky similar to Bourbon, which gives the final product a sweet aroma of vanilla so typical of that distillate.

Canadian distillers either blend their whisky immediately after it is distilled or after maturation. The barrels used for maturation may be new, or they may have been previously used for sherry, brandy or Bourbon. The law requires a minimum maturation period of three years, but the whisky is usually left to mature in the wood for at least four to five years.

How to recognise Canadian whisky – Blending is a vitally important operation for Canadian whisky, its components determining the final characteristics of the product. Nevertheless, the bitter, spicy taste of rye is present in all Canadian whiskies to a greater or lesser extent, depending on the amount of straight rye used in the

blending. At the same time, the aroma of vanilla which is typical of Bourbon reflects the amount used in blending.

As in Scotland, the price of Canadian whisky depends on the quantity of straight whisky used in blending it and on how many years it has matured in oak barrels. In Canada, too, the years of maturation given on the label refer to those of the "youngest" whisky in the blend. The high proportion of neutral alcohol used in the blending gives Canadian whisky a particularly light palate, while the malt rye gives it its characteristic sweetness.

JAPANESE WHISKY

The descendant of Scotch – There is no doubt whatsoever that Japanese whisky is directly descended from Scottish whisky. Japanese distilleries operate exactly like Scottish ones, using directly heated pot-stills for the double distillation of malt wort and continuous column stills for distilling of mixed grains. Often the malt used is imported from Scotland but the barley may also be imported from Australia, Europe or North America.

The Japanese also market some of their whiskies as single malt. But as in Scotland, most of the spirit produced is blended. In order to achieve a greater variety in their blends, Japanese distillers use malts imported directly from Scotland in proportions ranging between 12 and 15 per cent.

If the amount of malt whisky used in blending is more than 40 per cent, the resulting whisky is classified as a "super premium", while if it is between 35 and 40 per cent it is a "premium" whisky. "Special" whisky contains not less than 30 per cent. There are also whiskies classified as First and Second category, which contain at least 20 per cent and 10 per cent of malt respectively. These are sold mostly in supermarkets.

The greatest difference between Japanese and Scotch whisky lies in

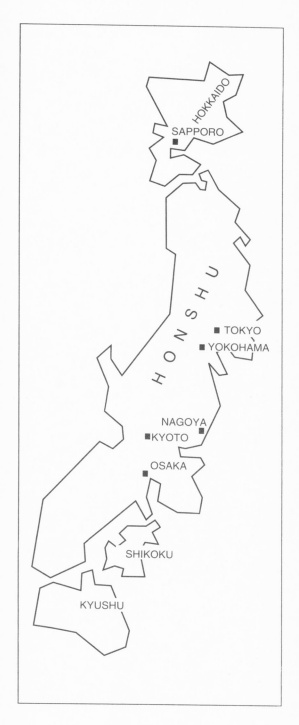

the use of peat which is less common in Japan than in Scotland. This means that the Japanese distillate has a less smoky fragrance, thus allowing the sweetness of the malt to come to the fore.

Maturation takes place in barrels which have previously contained sherry or Bourbon, or in new barrels of charred oak. As in Ireland and Scotland, the law in Japan requires a minimum maturation period of three years, but usually the distillate is left to mature for a much longer period. Indeed, some Japanese whiskies may be as much as twenty years old.

HOW TO
DRINK WHISKY

A very versatile companion

Whisk(e)y is a fascinating distillate whatever its provenance. The great variety of fragrances and aromas are, as we have seen, infinite. And it is not easy to find one's way in such a vast, complex universe. As always when talking of drink, the best criterion is that of personal taste without any preconceptions or snobbery. Whisky has an immense variety of flavours and complexity, represented by the large number of Scotch whisky blends and single malts, the American distillates, Irish whiskey and the Japanese blends. It is because of the large number of variables in its composition and manufacture that whisk(e)y is possibly the most versatile spirit ever invented by man. This is why it can be drunk on different occasions and for a range of purposes.

Although we would not want to interfere with individual freedom, nevertheless, as far as whisk(e)y is concerned, there is one rule which must always be followed. A single malt must never be allowed to mix with ice, soda or any other "companions". Single malt is a classic distillate which deserves reflection and thought: it should be savoured pure or diluted with a only little water. During the distillation process essential oils are produced and the water helps these to be released, thereby emphasising their aroma. The Scots say in fact that a single malt should be diluted with the same water that was used to produce it. This may well be true although it is obviously difficult to achieve in real life. Distilled water may be used, or one of the Scottish spring waters now available on the market. In any event, the amount of water used must never exceed that of the whisky. The most suitable glass to use for drinking a single malt whisky is the classic, tulip-shaped glass.

What is true of single malt Scotch also applies to Japanese single malts and Irish whiskey. But in the case of the latter, there are exceptions. Irish whiskey, with its distinctive character and unmistakable personality, has also become a "classic" when combined with coffee as Irish Coffee, and with chocolate and cream in liqueurs such as Irish Cream.

The situation is different in the case of blended whiskies, whatever

their provenance, which may be drunk with ice or used in cocktails or with mixers as long drinks. While a pure malt would tend to dominate all the components, a blended whisky will happily mix with other liquors. However, here too it is important to make a few distinctions. The regulations in the various whisky-making countries do not require manufacturers to state the percentages of malt and grain used in blending on the label. It is therefore impossible to know which distillates and in what quantities have been used in the blend. A little experience in the field can help one determine if the blend contains a high percentage of malt, and in that case one should be wary of mixing it; it might in fact be better to drink it neat or only with water.

The most suitable glass for whisky on the rocks is the tumbler, a large glass without a foot. Long drinks and cocktails can be drunk from a variety of glasses. Bourbon is often served in a tumbler with ice. But many Bourbons or full-bodied straight whiskies should rather be drunk neat or diluted only with water, which will enhance their fragrance.

As far as Canadian whisky is concerned, the lighter versions are perfect for long drinks, while fuller-bodied ones are very pleasant drunk neat or with ice and soda.

A useful word of advice for all types of whisky is that the bottles should be stored vertically. The spirit should never be in contact with the stopper.

RECIPES

Cheese Canapés

Ingredients: 450 g grated Swiss Emmenthal cheese; ½ cup Bourbon; 1 beaten egg; salt, pepper, paprika; 4 slices toast.
Mix together the cheese, Bourbon, egg, salt and pepper and spread the mixture on the slices of toast. Sprinkle paprika on top. Put in the oven until the cheese starts melting and turns golden. Serve immediately.

Bananas and Bacon in Bourbon

Ingredients: 3 bananas; a pinch of curry powder; juice of 1 lemon and 1 lime; 40 ml Bourbon; 6 slices bacon.

Cut the bananas in slices about 2 cm thick and sprinkle them with the curry powder. Allow to soak for at least one hour in the lemon juice, lime juice and Bourbon. Drain and wrap each piece of banana in a piece of bacon and secure with a cocktail stick. Put under the grill till the bacon is cooked.

Tagliatelle with Scotch

Ingredients: 50 g sultanas; 1 small glass Scotch whisky; 3 apples; ½ litre fresh cream; 3 egg yolks; butter; pinch of salt; ½ kg tagliatelle, cooked al dente.
Wash the sultanas and soak in Scotch whisky for a few hours. Peel the apples and cut into dice. Sauté them in a frying pan with a tablespoon of the butter and add the sultanas. As soon as the slices of apple start to turn golden, add the cream, mix it in well, then add the egg yolks and salt and mix again to bind all the ingredients together. Sauté the cooked tagliatelle with a little butter in a frying pan. As soon as the butter has been absorbed, add a small glass of Scotch, let it evaporate a little and add the sauce; stir well and serve.

Irish Risotto

Ingredients: 300 g minced beef; 1 stock cube; 3 yellow peppers; 6 desalted anchovies; 50 g butter; 1 small glass Irish whiskey; 400 g rice boiled al dente and well-drained.

Put the minced beef, stock cube, yellow peppers cut into fairly small pieces, and the desalted anchovies, also cut into small pieces, into the butter in a frying pan. When cooked add the Irish whiskey. Continue cooking until the whiskey has evaporated and the peppers have softened. Add the rice; leave to cook for a little longer so that the ingredients can bind together.

Cleikum Club Lobster

Ingredients: 1 fresh lobster, cut in two lengthways; 3 heaped tablespoons butter; salt and pepper; 4 teaspoons malt whisky; ¼ litre fresh cream.

Completely remove all the flesh from the lobster, including the head and the claws. Cut the lobster meat into fairly large pieces. Heat the butter and when it starts to foam, add the lobster, salt and pepper. Heat the whisky separately and when the lobster is hot pour the whisky on top and flame it. Add the cream, stirring it to deglaze the cooking juices, and heat gently, making sure the mixture does not come to the boil, thus preventing the cream from curdling. Fill the two empty halves of the lobster with this mixture and serve hot. Crabs, crayfish and scampi can all be prepared in this way.

(The Cleikum Club was a 19th-century Scottish society specialising in *haute cuisine*.)

Tweed Kettle

Ingredients: 1 kg fresh salmon; salt, pepper and nutmeg; 4 tablespoons Scotch whisky; 2 chopped shallots; 4 tablespoons fresh cream (if desired); 2 tablespoons chopped parsley.
Put the salmon in a pot and cover with cold water. Add salt, pepper and a pinch of nutmeg. Bring to the boil and continue cooking for just 5 minutes. Allow the salmon to cool down but do not throw away the broth. Clean the fish, removing the skin and the bones,

*and cut into fairly large cubes. Add a
little more salt, pepper and nutmeg,
then put everything in a saucepan with
a cup of the broth, all the whisky and
the shallots.*

Cover and allow to cook on a low
heat for approximately 25 minutes.
Now add the cream and warm up
without bringing it to the boil. Finally
garnish with parsley.

(Tweed Kettle was a speciality of
19th-century Edinburgh.)

Preserved Trout

*Ingredients: 12 trout; salt and pepper; 4
tablespoons Scotch whisky; 400 g
butter; 120 g white wine vinegar; pinch
of nutmeg and cloves.*

Clean the trout and remove the scales;
sprinkle with a little of the vinegar;
open the fish and remove all the bones.
Sprinkle inside and out with the salt
and pepper. Pour the whisky over the
fish and leave to marinade for a few
hours in a covered container. Place the
trout in an ovenproof dish with a knob
of the butter on each (200 g in all) and

sprinkle with the whisky marinade and a few spoonfuls of the remaining vinegar. Cover and cook in the oven at 100° C (210° F) for 45 minutes. Carefully remove from the cooking liquid and place on a clean dish. When they are cold, cover with the remaining butter, previously softened and mixed with the grated nutmeg and cloves. Serve cold. If well covered with butter and kept in a cool place, the trout will keep for several days. Herring and mackerel can be cooked in the same way.

Chicken with Honey, Whisky and Almonds

Ingredients: 1 chicken; 3 tablespoons whisky, preferably single malt; salt and pepper; 3 tablespoons thick honey; 60 g almonds, peeled and halved; 2 tablespoons oil.

Pour the whisky over the whole chicken and rub it so it penetrates the skin; sprinkle with salt and pepper. Take a piece of aluminium foil large enough to cover the bottom and sides of a casserole and also to cover the chicken. Place the chicken in the casserole and add the whisky. Spread the honey on the breast and legs, then put the almonds on top. Finally pour the oil inside the chicken. Seal well and cook in the oven at 180° C (350 F) for 75 to 90 minutes. Before serving, open up the aluminium envelope and brown under the grill for a few minutes.

Lamb with Pineapple

Ingredients: 2 double loin chops of lamb; 1 teaspoon dried mint; salt and pepper; 1 teaspoon butter; 2 slices of pineapple; 4 tablespoons Bourbon.

Heat the grill. Meanwhile make some cuts in the chops and slip the dried mint leaves inside. Season with salt and pepper and grill the meat at about 10 cm (4 in) from the source of the heat for 10 minutes on one side and for 6 on the other until both sides are golden and crisp (the inside will remain pink). During the last 5 minutes of cooking, heat up the butter in a frying pan, add the slices of pineapple and fry lightly on both sides. Place a chop on each of the two pineapple slices, sprinkle with the Bourbon, set light and serve flambé.

Peaches in a Syrup of Whisky

Ingredients: 16 yellow peaches;
450 g icing sugar; 1 litre water;
6 tablespoons whisky, preferably
single malt.
Place the peaches in a bowl and cover
with water. Leave for 5 minutes,
remove from the water and peel. Put
the sugar in the litre of water in a large
pan, bring to the boil and simmer for
about 15 minutes. Add the peaches,
bring back to the boil and continue to
simmer for another 15 minutes, stirring with a wooden spoon. Now put
the peaches in the serving bowl and
put the cooking syrup and whisky in a
pan and boil vigorously for 5 minutes.
When the mixture has cooled slightly,
pour over the peaches and put in the
fridge before serving.

Bourbon Bullets

Ingredients: 3 cups finely crushed
vanilla-flavoured wafer biscuits;
3 cups icing sugar; 1½ teaspoons cocoa;
1½ cups ground walnuts; 3 tablespoon
golden syrup; ½ cup Bourbon.
Mix all the ingredients together and

make small bullets about 2.5 cm (1 in) in diameter; sprinkle them with icing sugar. Serve immediately, or having chilled them in the fridge.

These quantities will make about 40 bullets.

Atholl Brose

Ingredients: 3 heaped tablespoons oatmeal flour; 2 tablespoons liquid heather honey; ¾ bottle Scotch whisky.

Put the oatmeal in a bowl and mix with some water added bit by bit to obtain a firm dough. Allow to rest for 1 hour and then put the mixture through a fine sieve, pressing hard with a spoon to drain the mixture. Throw away the oatmeal and mix the filtered water with the honey using a silver spoon.

Pour into a 750-ml bottle and fill it up with Scotch. Seal well and shake before serving.

Although Atholl Brose is traditionally consumed as a drink it can also be turned into a delicious dessert in the following manner. Using goblets or stemmed glasses, put 1 tablespoon of the mixture in each glass and top with sweetened whipped cream. Sprinkle with a little toasted oatmeal and a dusting of nutmeg. Serve cold with amaretti.

Irish Coffee

This book had to finish with a classic, and from the many recipes for Irish Coffee we have chosen this one, transcribed by an Irishman so that there is no doubt about its originality:

"Cream – thick as an Irish shoe; coffee – strong as the hand of a friend; sugar – sweet as the tongue of a vagabond; whiskey – soft as the spirit of the moors".

Heat a goblet of about 180 ml in hot water, then pour about 40 ml of Irish whiskey into it. Add 3 small cubes of sugar. Fill the goblet with steaming hot black coffee. Stir well, then add the cream by running it over the back of a spoon so that it floats. The cream can be liquid or lightly whipped.

Bibliography

Various authors, *Scotch Whisky*, London, Macmillan, 1979.

P. Colacicchi, *Il libro del whisky*, Milan, Mursia, 1971.

D. Daiches, *Scotch Whisky*, 1972.

L. Ferrari, *Dublino chiama whiskey, Edimburgo risponde whisky*, in *Il barman*, Milan, Dilettoso & Co., May 1987.

E. and M. Greenberg, *Guida internazionale alle varietà di liquori*, Bologna, Nuova Ulisse Edizioni, 1992.

E. Guagnini and F. Zingales, *Il whisky*, Firenze, Sansoni, 1978.

M. Jackson, *The World Guide to Whisky*, London, Dorling Kindersley, 1987.

M. Magee, *1000 Years of Irish Whiskey*, Dublin, The O'Brien Press, 1980.

P. Morrice, *Guida allo Scotch Whisky*, Milan, Dilettoso & Co., 1986.

M. Moss and J. Hume, *The Making of Scotch Whisky*, Edinburgh, 1981.

L. Odello, *Irish Whiskey*, in *Il barman*, op. cit., September 1987.

L. Odello, *L'alambicco americano e i suoi figli*, in *Il barman*, op. cit., November 1987.

L. Odello, *Per un giorno blender*, in *Il barman*, op. cit., June 1987.

L. Odello, *Una giornata da ... super malti!*, in *Il barman*, op. cit., July 1987

L. Odello, *Whisky & Whiskey*, Brescia, Edizioni AEB, 1986.

ACKNOWLEDGEMENTS

The author thanks her friend and colleague Franco Zingales for the important contribution which he has made to the writing of this book. An affectionate thank you also to Simone Giorgi and Alessio Turchi.

110

INDEX

113

114

The Connoisseur's Companions

Also in the series:

Chocolate

Delicious and simple-to-make recipes and quirky anecdotes are just a small part of this charming gift book for the chocolate lover.

Coffee

A vast expanse of information about the timeless beverage that is coffee; a compact guide to a complex ingredient.

Olive Oil

Olive oil has become the single most important ingredient in cooking today. Also featuring delicious recipes, this is a useful, concise, easy-to-follow guide.